Grandma's Buried Treasure

By Christine Leger

Mia and Leo loved visiting Grandma more than anything. Every summer, for one whole week, they got to stay at her cozy little house, a place filled with the smell of cookies and the sound of Grandma's gentle humming. This year felt extra special.

But on the second day, the sky grumbled with thunder, and fat raindrops began to splat against the windows. "Oh bother," sighed Mia, looking out at the downpour. "What will we ever do inside all day?" Grandma smiled. "Well, my dears, have you ever explored the attic?"

The attic was a treasure trove! Dust motes danced in the shafts of sunlight that peeked through the cracks in the roof. Old trunks overflowed with forgotten clothes, chipped teacups lined shelves, and stacks of yellowed books leaned against the walls. It smelled like sunshine and old secrets. Mia immediately started rummaging through a trunk filled with hats, while Leo explored a dusty collection of tools.

"Wow, check this out!" Leo called, holding up a tarnished telescope. Mia placed a feathered hat on her head and twirled around, giggling.

Suddenly, Mia stopped twirling. "Leo, look!" she exclaimed, pointing to a rolled-up piece of paper tied with a faded ribbon. It was tucked inside an old, leather-bound journal. Carefully, she untied the ribbon and unfurled the paper. It was a map! A hand-drawn map, filled with winding paths and curious markings.

"What is it?" Leo asked, peering over her shoulder.

The words "Dove Woods Mystery Trail" were written in elegant script at the top. "Dove Woods! That's right behind Grandma's house!" Mia exclaimed. Leo noticed something else. "Wait a minute," he said, pointing to a particular swirl in the drawing. "That looks like Grandma's handwriting!" A thrill of excitement ran through them. Could this be a secret trail Grandma had created?

They hurried downstairs, the map clutched tightly in Mia's hand. "Mom! Mom! Look what we found in the attic!" They burst into the kitchen, where their mom was humming as she stirred a pot on the stove. She knelt down, took the map, and smiled. "Well, well, well. Looks like Grandma left you something special to discover."

"Can we go? Can we go now?" Mia pleaded, bouncing on the balls of her feet. Mom chuckled. "Of course, you can go. But promise me you'll stay together, and don't forget the cookies! Grandma packed them for a reason, you know." Mia gave their Mother a big hug and took some cookies

With cookies in tow, Mia grabbed the adventure hat she always brought on her camping trips, and Leo slung his trusty explorer bag over his shoulder. They raced out the back door and into the woods. Dove Woods wasn't very big, but it was filled with towering trees, babbling brooks, and the sweet song of birds. The map was their guide, leading them down a narrow, winding trail.

The map was like a treasure map, taking them through the woods with hand-written notes and wooden signs. "Turn left at the tree with the curly branch!" Mia read out loud. They looked left and right, trying to find the curly branch. "You're almost there, Brave Explorers!" Leo noticed.

Deeper into the woods they went, finding little treasures along the way. Tucked in a tree hollow, they found a faded photograph of baby Mia wearing a flower crown. A note from Grandma was attached, reading, "You loved this spot when you were little!" Then, hanging from a low branch, they found a colorful kite with a tag that said, "For breezy days with big imaginations."

"Oh, I remember this kite!" Mia giggled. "Grandma used to run with me in the meadow, trying to get it to fly." Leo smiled. "She's the best Grandma ever." The trail twisted and turned, leading them deeper and deeper into the heart of Dove Woods. Every twist and turn felt like a secret waiting to be discovered.

Finally, they reached the big red 'X' marked on the map. It was under a shady oak tree, its trunk gnarled and old. A knot in the wood was shaped like a perfect heart. "This is it!" Leo exclaimed. They knelt down, peering beneath the moss and fallen leaves. And there it was – a painted wooden box!

With trembling hands, they lifted the lid. Inside, nestled on a bed of soft cloth, was a collection of family photos: Grandma, Grandpa, Mom as a kid, and even pictures of baby Leo and Mia. There were little notes written just for them. One said, "You're clever, kind, and always curious. That's a real treasure!"

And that wasn't all! There was a jump rope, a box of sidewalk chalk, a magnifying glass, a whistle, and a small flag that read "Brave Trail Twins HQ." Leo picked up the flag, grinning. "This is amazing!" Mia read the last note. "This trail was made just for you—so you'll always know how much you're loved. See you next summer!" It was signed "Love, Grandma."

As the sun began to set, they carried the box home, their hearts full of joy. They were tired but glowing. Mom smiled as they unpacked the treasures on the porch. "Your grandma knew you'd find it. She always had a way of making summers extra special."

That night, as the stars twinkled above, Mia and Leo sat on the porch, sketching in their notebooks. "Next year," Mia said, "Let's make a new map for Grandma! A mystery trail just for her!" Leo nodded, a mischievous glint in his eyes. "With even more secret clues!" They smiled, imagining new adventures in Dove Woods, creating memories to pass on for generations to come.

www.ingramcontent.com/pod-product-compliance
Lightning Source LLC
Chambersburg PA
CBHW081012120626
46546CB00010B/3125